How Wally Lost His Thumb and the Boy Scouts Became Cannibals

New & Selected Poems
by Al Ortolani

Kansas City   Spartan Press   Missouri

Spartan Press
Kansas City, Missouri
spartanpresskc.com

Copyright (c) Al Ortolani, 2018
First Edition 1 3 5 7 9 10 8 6 4 2
ISBN: 978-1-946642-88-2
LCCN: 2018965477

Design, edits and layout: Jason Ryberg
Cover Art, *Murmuration,* by Jacque Forsher, Dallas, Texas.
Title page image: unknown photographer (according to author).
Author photos: Sherri Ortolani
All rights reserved. No part of this publication may be
reproduced or transmitted in any form or by any means,
electronic or mechanical, including photocopying,
recording or by info retrieval system, without prior
written permission from the author.

Acknowledgements:

Thanks to Gary Lechliter, Kevin Rabas, and Alarie Tennille for their careful attention to these poems, as well as to Jason Ryberg and Spartan Press for their dedication to the written word. Special thanks to J.T. Knoll for the line which I stole, "jail as a monastery with razor wire," to my wife Sherri, the cowboys, and to Steve, I hope you found your thumb. If not, I think it's on the railroad tracks.

Townes Van Zandt quotation from the American Songwriter, The Craft of Music, an article by Holly Gleason.
http://americansongwriter.com/2010/01/legends-townes-van-zandt/holly

The author would like to thank the editors of the following journals and presses where many of these poems, sometimes in different versions, first appeared.

Amaryllis Poetry: "Roseland Road House," "Wally Sings Amazing Grace in an Arkansas Cave"
Boston Literary Magazine: "Wally Recalls Maslow's Hierarchy"
The Chiron Review: "Wally Practices Pranayama at the Self-Serve"
Coal City Poetry Review: "War Trophy"
The English Journal: "How Wally Lost His Thumb and the Boy Scouts Became Cannibals"
Eunoia Review: "Bracket for Normal"
The Galway Review: "Wally Dismisses His Midlife Crises by Shooting an Inanimate Object"
In Between Hangovers: "Maurice's New Age Revolution Began in a Pickup Truck," "Sparrows Fly Home," "Wally Ate an Electric Hot Dog at a Rock Festival"
I-70 Review: "White High Tops"
Mead: The Magazine of Literature and Libations: "Highway Signs Are Painted Green"

The New Mexico Poetry Review: "No Account Gordon"
The Orange Room Review: "Hitching by Night across New Mexico"
Picaroon Poetry: "The Day Wally Was Murdered Love Poem"
The Quarterly: "After Johnny's Overdose Wally Walks in Pretending to be Retarded," "Boys Dig Through the Neighbor's Trash Only to be Beset by Great Mystery," "Double Dating with Wally," "Frisbee Investigates the Angle of Love," "Mama DeBeauty Explains a Necessary But Uncomfortable Aspect of Dude Ranching"
Red River Poetry Review: "Wally Steals Oscar the Lab Skeleton"
Softblow: "Wally Recalls Fortune Hunting"
Strange Poetry: "Screwing the Pooch"
Turtle Island Quarterly: "After the Book Release Party, Wally Walks Down 39th Street with a Box on His Head"
The Yellow Ham: "Wally's Professor Busts a Local Meth Lab," "While Taking Tickets at the Drive-In Theater, Wally Discovers the Cost of Chivalry"

Some of the poems in this collection also appeared in:

Finding the Edge, Woodley Press
Waving Mustard in Surrender, NYQ Books
Paper Birds Don't Fly, NYQ Books

As the Wally collection grew, I decided early on to include them in whatever chronological collection of poems they fit into. Much of this had to do with the hope that inspiration for the Wally series would continue. However, I was never sure when or if they would stop. In putting this New & Selected collection together, I gathered many of the poems that fit Wally's story, changing where need be the occasional name or detail that helped the series congeal as a single piece. Wally is a work of fiction as are many of our "best laid plans."

TABLE OF CONTENTS

Crayon Sucker

Crayon Sucker / 1

Anything for Susie / 2

White High Tops / 4

The Double Dog / 6

Straight Talk / 7

Wally Recalls Fortune Hunting / 8

No Account Gordon / 9

How Wally Lost His Thumb and the Boy Scouts
    Became Cannibals / 11

Wally and the Boy Scouts Study Poverty on a
    Missouri Highway / 13

As if War Was Inevitable, Wally Decides to Test
    the Secret Weapon / 15

War Trophy / 17

Baby Boom Schnauzer / 19

The Petrified Cowboy / 21

Boys Dig Through Neighbor's Trash Only to
    Become Beset by Great Mystery / 22

Mama DeBeauty Explains a Necessary But
    Uncomfortable Aspect of Dude Ranching / 24

Double Dating with Wally / 26

The Great Night with Cowboys / 28

While Taking Tickets at the Drive-In Theater,
    Wally Discovers the Cost of Chivalry / 30

Wally and the Cowboys Drive across
    Low Water Bridge in High Water / 32
Frisbee Investigates the Angle of Love / 34
Roseland Road House / 36

Crow

Cousin Once Removed / 39
How Crows Find Themselves / 46
How Crows Get By / 49
How Crows Dissolve / 51
Crow Remembers Cigar Bands / 53
Fourteen Lines for Raymond Lee / 55
A Flat Line of Crows Is Still a Murder / 56
Crow's Small Wild / 57
Snow Dusts a Crow / 58

Oscar the Lab Skeleton

Old Girlfriend at Crow's Funeral / 61
After Johnny's Drug Overdose Wally Keeps
    His Memory Alive by Begging Cookies
    at Truck Stops / 62
After Graduation Wally Rummages in the Strip Pits / 65
Wally Steals Oscar the Lab Skeleton / 67
Wally Ate an Electric Hot Dog at a Rock Festival / 69
Gordon's New Age Revolution Began
    in a Pickup Truck / 71
Sparrows Fly Home / 72
Charlie Miller Burns One / 73

Wally Falls Asleep During Meditation
    Only to be Awakened by a Home Invasion / 74
At Night, Wally Imagines the County Jail
    as a Monastery with Razor Wire / 76
Hitching by Night across New Mexico / 77
Wally Reads His Second Hand Bly at the DMV / 78
Mockingbird / 79
Last Float Trip with Wally and the Hobbits / 80
Highway Signs Are Painted Green / 81
The Day Wally Was Murdered Love Poem / 82
Wally Dismisses Crises by Shooting
    an Inanimate Object / 84
After the Book Release Party,
    Wally Walks Down 39th Street
    with a Box on His Head / 85
Old Boy / 86
Wally's Professor Busts a Local Meth Lab / 87
The After Midnight Supermarket / 88

Dancing at the American Legion

Vietnam Was Once / 93
Screwing the Pooch / 96
The Hat Trick / 99
Wally Recalls Maslow's Hierarchy / 100
Prayer Feet / 102
Dancers at the American Legion / 104
Wally Practices Pranayama at the Self-Serve / 105
Wally Sings Amazing Grace in an Arkansas Cave / 106
The Starving Mule / 108
Wally Smokes a Cigar with Sam Clemens / 110

In Memoriam:

Dr. Dana Alan Cope
Paleoanthropologist, Dog Lover
Prince of Hedge Apples

*There's only two kinds of music:
the blues and zippety doo-dah.*

—Townes Van Zandt

Crayon Sucker

Crayon Sucker

Even as a boy
Wally took issue with good advice.
Frequently, his teachers
kept a desk for him up front
near the chalkboard. His classmates
expected entertainment.
He ate their enthusiasm.
He rehearsed funny faces at himself
in the mirror, sucked on
purple crayons like cigars,
ate paste from a gallon jar,
construction paper from the top
of his desk. He drew pictures
of great battles on the back of his
math assignments, complete
with sounds effects, bombs, missiles,
machine guns, soldiers screaming.
At conferences, the counselor
said he was a real people person.
Teachers regaled his untapped potential.
His parents learned to accept Cs
from their above average,
crayon sucking child.

Anything for Susie

When I was four
this lovely girl combed
her golden hair against
her red lapel,

stroked it in place
with her palm, while asking me
in the same breath to crawl
into Splinter's plywood

dog house. I did.
I climbed inside, not knowing why,
snagging my cap on nails, pushing my
hands through the mildewed

dog pissy straw. As soon
as my feet cleared the sill,
she slapped the door shut, shoved
out the light, and latched me in

with the spiders and the fleas.
When I rattled the door,
she giggled. When I kicked
with the heels of my new

western boots, she laughed,
and when I cried, she said
ok baby wait a minute
and she jiggled the latch.

When I quieted, wiped
away the tears and snot with a sleeve,
she cracked the door
and her demon dog Splinters

bolted in, chasing
circles around my face,
my hands whirling, winnowing
the straw. The dust rose in my throat,

a gag that I hocked
but forced myself to swallow.

White High Tops

There is a hollow space
under the hedge that we
squirm through, the Smith's
old bitch of a dog growling,
snapping at our heels from
the end of her leash. Billy
Clay is just ahead of me,
his butt so high that it
keeps snagging branches.
The dog strains, grabs
the toe of my Converse.
I kick her in the snout
with my free foot. She
shakes her wooly head,
pulls harder. The shoe
is important to me, new,
a gift on Christmas. Jesus,
I punch Billy Clay
in the ass. He's crying
like a baby. Christ,
I kick the dog three times
in the head. These are
my new shoes. There won't
be another pair until
Easter, if ever. The dog's

grip loosens, only
a shoestring caught in
his upper canine. I shove
Billy with my head
through the hedge. He
smells like piss, blubbering
in the sun, a swollen leaking
inner tube of a boy. The rubber
toe of my left converse
is shredded, even my sock
torn. I slug Billy
in the stomach and
he doubles at the waist.
Look at my shoe, I cry.
My life is ruined.

The Double Dog

     One afternoon
I pulled a beauty of a wheelie
on Anna Merkin's street
and the front wheel fell off.
The only way
I could keep the forks
from the impending catastrophe
was to pedal faster; it was
a temporary solution at best.
Later, the same summer,
Wally filled his handlebars
with gasoline so he could ride
a rocket through her neighborhood.
After the explosion, his father
smacked the fire out of him.
On a double dog, we rubbed
our genitals with poison ivy.
Friends visited us at home,
grew transfixed by our courage,
our slathered calamine.

Straight Talk

One of the boys said I'd go to hell
after Charlie Miller and I had dropped
our pants, and in a moment of hilarity
had crossed swords.
It was the sin of Adam and Eve,
the boy said, being naked outside
in the Miller's back yard in front
of God and baseball and summer trees.
I'd never heard of such a sin.
I knew about Adam and Eve. I knew
they'd fucked up something fierce. I knew
they walked around wearing nothing
but leaves. Sister Plum, my spiritual advisor,
had only mentioned the apple
of their sin. She'd called it original.
Somehow this made sense of my guilt.
No one I knew went around naked
in the backyard. No one crossed swords.
Apple or no apple, I couldn't go to my mother.
So I asked Wally. He was at least fourteen,
smoked cigarettes, knew as much
as a magazine on these things.
Wally and I watched a June bug negotiate
a crack in the front steps. Finally,
he said, the thing is—you never know
what you shouldn't know
until you know it.

Wally Recalls Fortune Hunting

Yoyos, hula hoops, pet rocks—
once as a 4th grader, I side-armed
a flat rock at the class tyrant; it
slid through the afterschool air
like a spinning plate before cold-
cocking him in the side of the head.
He dropped like a bag of laundry.
I'd never seen a Frisbee before,
but I should have known
I was onto something. His mother
called my mother and said that I
was of all things, a bully. I hadn't
considered that before. I was the
smallest kid in the fourth grade.
I thought of myself more
as an opportunist, an inventor.
But the tyrant found me alone that summer
walking barefoot in the grass
along Ohio Street. He pushed me
onto the hot pavement where the tar
sizzled and popped in the summer sun.
Every time I danced to the curb,
he shoved me back into the street.
Paybacks are inevitable, but shoes,
I should have thought of that.

No Account Gordon

The baby Jesus was a rubber doll,
one whose eyes would flip open when you lifted him
and drop closed when you laid him flat.

The manger was a toy crib
or a painted cardboard box.
It didn't matter in 5th grade,
since drama was art, and art was taught
every Friday after lunch, and
according to Sister, the baby Jesus
could be found in anything anywhere anytime,
and was certainly no illusion, no way no how.

Gordon, however, bounced a basketball
from the moment he left home
until he entered
the school playground. Then he stood
where the four-square courts were painted

and dribbled even more.

In November, when Sister cast the Christmas play,
he was chosen to be
one of the three wise men, a real Magi,
aloof, star-gazing, accountable only
to his inner vision.

He moved in December
to Phoenix, a faraway, desert place.
We didn't see him again until high school,
when he returned to town
essentially unrecognizable
in his black leather jacket,
Beatle boots and tight jeans. The boys
traded him high-fives.
The girls, who thought him weird in grade school,
saw him as dark and mysterious
with his wonderfully banged hair,
his wise lips, his open
kiss me Jesus eyes.

How Wally Lost His Thumb
and the Boy Scouts Became Cannibals

We had fought
for hours over the
cooking of the stew,
wrestling in the yellow
hay like denim clad
cubs. Until Wally
in a fit of ambition
whittled a chunk
from his favorite thumb.
It was a masterful cleave
with a well-whetted blade
and an inspirational heave

that chucked the thumb
thick into the pan
of sizzling ham,
where as quickly as spit
it curled and fizzled
into an unidentifiable
hunk of gristle

awfully comparable
to dinner.
So, of course, here lay
the quandary:

to dismiss the ham
into the autumn turned leaves
or let it all fry
down into the sumptuous
fat we'd planned.

Amid curled pork,
slices of onion, potatoes
and sliver of thumb,
a dozen eggs were dumped,
and when at last
the plates were mopped
and the spatula cleaned,

the thumb
garnished with salt
and a little pepper
had been nibbled down
or swallowed whole.
From that day on
it became apparent
a cannibal was among us
a boy scout within us.

Wally and the Boy Scouts Study Poverty on a Missouri Highway

A half a dozen hardscrabble shacks
lay back of the old highway, nearly
hidden behind the trees. Tar paper,
peeling plywood, corrugated tin.

Still too visible from the new road
connecting Joplin to Pittsburg. The Boy Scouts
hiked too near on their way to camp
that summer. A skillet of dirt-smeared

boys materialized out of the trees, tossed
rocks from the safety of a ditch. The scouts
kept their arms over their heads, watched
for some adult from inside
to yank a leash, and rein the wildness

out of them. Rocks pelted the scouts for
fifty-yards until they started up the hill
to the new road, then the barrage stopped.
Charlie Miller picked up a flat rock

to skip back. The scoutmaster said, Drop it.
Keep walking. I suppose it was a lesson
in nonviolence, or in leaving poverty

as it lay, a stone unturned, a don't-blame-them-
for-hating-you moment.
But one way or another, the scouts saw
no merit badge in walking away,
or for throwing rocks at poor kids.

As if War Was Inevitable, Wally Decides to Test the Secret Weapon

Wally knew we were coming
stalking diagonally up
the branches, testing and
twisting through the leaves
to the tree house where
he waited on the plywood platform.
When we got halfway,
he stood
and peed, the yellow
stream splattering
above our heads, spraying
off the branches onto
our hands and arms
and faces. We screamed,
slipping down the
way we'd come like insects
in a rain. A heavy
deluge caught Mike
between the shoulder blades,
splattering his T-shirt
like machine gun fire.
Mike fell
dropping into a pile of
discarded lumber.

Wally pinched his last
three squirts in our
direction. We held
close to the main trunk,
the yellow fire streaming
over our heads. Bill
slipped and hung by one hand,
his knuckles white
and beaded with yellow.
It works Wally hollered.
and the boys cheered.

War Trophy

When Mr. Madden wheeled his bright
Pontiac into the driveway,
we were on the roof of his house—

faces pressed to the window.
The house was an irresistible trespass
buried in the trees like a pillbox.

Madden wouldn't kill us (only our fathers
had that right), but he would
gun us down with his salt-filled

12 gauge. Joey (they said) had been
blown spread eagled into
a barbed wire fence. It had taken

days for his blisters to heal.
No one denied it. There were rumors—
of skulls, Nazi helmets, splendid

daggers, an Iron Cross.

Old Madden, one leg on the floorboards,
the other planted in gravel, shook
his fist like a club. Wally and I jumped—

parachutists with knees bent,
rolling into Normandy. My brother,
only six, wept as he struggled

down the ladder. On the roof where
I had pushed my nose to the glass,
I'd seen an end table with a lamp,

an embroidered doily, and
a framed black and white
of a woman with a girl and a dog.

My brother lost his shoe as we fled.
The old man turned it in his hand.
He lobbed it after us, a grenade

like we'd seen in the movies.

Baby Boom Schnauzer

One afternoon Uncle Raymond's son,
a cousin once removed,
(whom the neighbor's thought crazy
since he liked to dress up
like a Nazi), threatened to kill my mother.
I don't remember why.
I was too young for death threats,
but I felt responsible
since he was a boy and I was a boy.
Mother kept calling him *my friend*
as she told the story to her step-father
who came from across town
to sit on the couch by the window.

I loved my friend's dagger
and Nazi helmet. They were for real.
He smoked cigarettes and showed off
blisters on his forearms from burn-outs
in the back seats of cars.
He told me frightening stories about sex.
I discovered later that he was
anatomically correct in his descriptions,
but emotionally, a schnauzer.
I began having anxiety attacks
in the months that followed.
I steered clear of confrontations.

At night, I wet the bed
and dreamed of Nazis. It was all
too complicated for a ten-year-old.
My father's job kept him on the road,
so, I watched reruns of *Combat*.
Sergeant Saunders knew how to pull the trigger.
I borrowed a plastic
Thompson machine gun
from Miller's little brother.
Some nights I sat on the edge of my bed
and held it under the crook of my arm
like Saunders did. One night
my friend walked out of his house
in full Nazi regalia. I lifted the window
with the barrel of the Thompson
and shot the shit out of him.
He fell under the streetlight,
his helmet clanking against the curb,
and that should have been the end of it.

The Petrified Cowboy

Death had not reached them
standing at the edge of the carnival
between the reptile tank and the two headed calf.
The boys were unspent,
feeling lucky and new,
as if they held the one ball that could
topple the proverbial three bottles.

It was this unused and unspoken self
that drew them to the tent where the dead cowboy lay,
encased in glass, more a manikin
than a man, claw hands,
sewn eyes, skin shriveled and shining like a wallet.

Ten cents.

The barker shuffled them in and let them gape, railing
about Texas deserts, Egyptian mummies and high
   mountain caves
but refusing to let them lift the glass. Afterwards
they sat below the city oaks,
confused by the price of truth.
They batted acorns with a stick,
pretending baseball,
popping called shots into the green pond.

Boys Dig Through Neighbor's Trash
Only to Become Beset by Great Mystery

Why did the neighbor
sisters wrap their

used Kotex
in aluminum foil
and store them
all away
in an oversized
burlap-colored suitcase,
leaving them on the back
porch when they moved?

What led Wally and I,
snooping as boys do
after a neighbor moves,
to swoop through
their belongings like
two gusts of spring wind?
Was it this find that later
drew Wally into anthropology
to dig
through equally mysterious ruins
for tampons of
the Anasazi, and maxi-pads
of Amazons?

What became of the Mayans?
Did they evolve elaborate
astronomical calendars, only
to have them defined
with a period?
Did Atlanteans use string?

And to what do I owe my poetry,
if not to the inspired flow
of the Muses, the great mystery
of the female, opened to me
at such a green age,
wrapped in shining foil,
bearing the blood of life.

Mama DeBeauty Explains a Necessary But Uncomfortable Aspect of Dude Ranching

Darla and Allison DeBeauty
were fine looking sisters.
They lived in the small
green rental
on Dakota Street
and never quite shut
their blinds.

I could get on Wally's
shoulders and we'd
stagger from window to
bedroom window,
hoping for a chance
to glimpse something pink.

One Sunday evening, moments
before Bonanza, Wally
caught his foot in a
gopher hole and fell against
the side of the house
so hard
it rattled the kitchen china.

Well, when Mama DeBeauty
nabbed us by the earlobes
and shook us

against the clapboard
until our gonads
rattled like little seed gourds,
I pointed to Wally
and said in shaken desperation,

*My friend's in love
with your daughter.*
Well, that changed everything.
Just as quickly as Little Joe
could mount his pony,
she had us seated
in the living room
and proceeded to show us

photos of her father's
dude ranch with stall after stall
of well-mannered geldings.

Double Dating with Wally

    Well, he was smart.
He understood his role.
He'd tell girls flat, I'm everything
you were ever
warned about in Driver's Ed.
I drink and smoke and show
off in intersections,
race trains, do donuts,
and refuse to yield
the right-of-way.
I'm a son of a bitch at the wheel
and seldom in touch
with reality.

Well, the girls would start
screaming and begging him to stop
but Wally was off,
blown into one of those crazy moods
to which he was prone,
what with homegrown and malt
and females pretending to be helpless,
so it all added up
to burying the speedometer
in the scream of the road,
beating a lucky guess
through Five Mile Corner
and yelping out of the window
like he was calling to the moon.

Eventually, he'd stop, pull
off roadside and want to know
what all the fuss was about,
and the girls would say you're
crazy crazy crazy
and we're getting out so we
can live a while longer.
And Wally would sadden and promise,
really promise to drive like he cared.
Because he was wrong and sorry
and his little brother was all crippled and
lived in a wheelchair and could
only put picture puzzles into whole pictures.

So they'd feel something sorry and stay
and he'd kick it
back into gear and tear ninety
towards Columbus, following
Highway 7 towards the horizon line,
laughing and laughing like he was
crazy crazy crazy,
and they'd cry, pounding on his arm,
you promised you wouldn't,
you promised.

The Great Night with Cowboys

Edward was in love
with fun and when
Wally threw him
onto the floor of the
Sad Song Bar, he kicked the tip
of his western boot
into Wally's groin.
Wally crumpled into
the lap of Junior Ash.
Junior yelled fag, threw
a bottle at one of
the laughing Simpson brothers
and clipped a redneck
they called Ace.

At that point Sally Ann screamed
fingers got smashed, cheeks
gashed and one girl
had her bra unsnapped.
When the bouncers elbowed
Charlotte into a balcony post,

Ace lost his mind and
ground one gorilla into the floor boards.

The other was
stuffed in a urinal
by a crowd chanting, *We love Ace.*
So really, nothing was unusual
with the Sad Song crowd.

Later, when the sheriff showed
and unloaded a round of tear gas
through the windows,
Edward and Wally cried,
but not for lack of fun.

While Taking Tickets at the Drive-In Theater, Wally Discovers the Cost of Chivalry

One night this cowboy
wheels in to the Drive-In
with his headlights pointing
skyward to the moon, rear end
clipping speed bumps, muffler
dragging. Wally is taking tickets
below the marquee, so he steps
up to the window to get the money
but there's no one in the car,
except a skinny-assed driver
surrounded by a dozen voices
escaping from the headliner,
the air vent, the ashtray,
the cigarette lighter,
all speaking crazy-fast
in something like Spanish
or Comanche.

      Wally thinks about you
Miss Ticket Girl in the mini skirt,
perched on your stool by the cash drawer.
The driver smiles, and Wally takes his cash,
pretending like he doesn't see the scam.
What if he challenges? And the trunk latch

clicks and a dozen tough guys
from the road crew climb out
with stilettos and switch blades
and shining white teeth, and what if
they only have enough money between them
for one popcorn and a drink. Think about it,
what if the two of you
would have to chip in, buy all those tough guys
tickets, popcorn and root beer? And then,
you'd have to sit with them
through an entire spaghetti western.
You in the backseat. Wally in the trunk.

Wally and the Cowboys Drive Across Low Water Bridge in High Water

Even as the creek washed
across the hood, hydroplaning
the body of the old Ford
downstream, they believed
in the dead engine, the headlights
submerged, illuminating
the curling flood,
the flight of perch.
There was a tingle
near the base
of their spines, a sudden
gush of adrenalin, a bitch slap
into the face of minimum
wage. The Ford settled, tires
touched concrete, the bridge
finding them again. The water of
Cow Creek rolled back
on itself to the door panels,
the edge of the bridge yawning
a saucer of white foam. One by one
they squeezed through the windows,
dropped into the winter water,
wading knee-deep like penitents
to the shore. Now,

the rain came again,
lashing their faces
like whips. They turned into it,
breathed for the first time
all week.

Frisbee Investigates the Angle of Love

When Frisbee's girlfriend
chose a woman to be her lover
instead of him,
he flipped
and took to driving
over to Galena and
jumping off of the chat
piles. He had a mathematical mind

and could calculate
the number of bounces
it would take
to keep
a fall from killing him.

He'd jump without fanfare,
unceremoniously,
slowing his descent
by bouncing
from ridge to ridge,

scuffing the gravel
into dozens of scraping
avalanches,
with all of us

looking on as silently
as plants,
assuming he'd lost
his mind as well as
his cherry,

in awe how that girl
must have been one soft cookie
to create

such a crumbling,
setting him up
to climb again
to the lip of the slope, and
before jumping, to mumble aloud,

Maybe, I'll get it right this time.

Roseland Road House

You left me after I was
knocked to the dance floor
by a boy with storied knuckles, more
seasoned, more muscled than I,
one of many who couldn't hold
your gaze. As I was shuffled
from the back door, supported
by two of my friends,
I wish you had followed me
into the parking lot, and explained
the gap between us.
Anything would have sufficed,
even a lie, a story about the man
I was trying to become.

Crow

Cousin Once Removed

(johnny crow, arrested for vandalism)

after daddy ray-man
walked out on momma for good
i took a hammer and busted up
car windows down at the lot
where he sold the pieces of shit

the minister called my momma
and brought her down to where
the sheriff had me — he patted
my arm all gentle and told momma
there but for the grace of god

mostly, i get it now, luck of the irish,
but where does that get me now,
dumb as a truck,
a leaf plowed under

(johnny crow works on the truck)

i got the breather clean
on the pickup truck, it balances
like a pan on the carburetor

if i rev the engine hard
one punch more than i should
it kicks off and flips
off the fan into the blue eye
of the sky — there it twirls
and spins for some minutes

until clangin against the garage floor
spent and collapsed to concrete
like a man
done with lovin

(johnny crow names his dog)

the judge says, johnny crow
you have a streak of cruelty
and i do not see you comin
to a good end — i nod
turnin my eyes down to my
boot toes — probation too
good for you, he whacks
the hammer hard — it is ringin
in my ear still

streak of cruelty
is the name i give my old dog
he doesn't know any different

he comes by any name
that be attached to food—
i yells here you be streak
but he sulks off between
some alley fences,
waitin me to leave his bowl

i drop it near the door
where i can wait behind the screen—
when streak of cruelty shows
thinkin he can get somethin
for nothin, I think to toss him this bone
sidearm at his head

but that would be like punchin
myself in the nose
twice

(johnny crow visits the library)

i come in sometime just to think
about all them words
pressed like a little a boy's flowers

i run my finger over line after line

i move my mouth so the lady at the desk
will think it's not just tobacco

i'm chewin — the words like crowfeet
jump up and down the branch
without much sense

(johnny crow takes his boy to school)

skinny boy of my son
goes to school — i watch him
join with the others, packin smiles
like he belongs — but i know inside
he isn't nothin more than
a pushin force
wantin to bust free

like me always turnin over the new leaf
maples elms oaks sweet gums,
a weepin willow more like it — other boys shove
my boy around just to hear him crow,

he needs to learn to toughen up,
see that guff for what it is,
and slap one of their heads
into the cyclone fence

my boy got little business
bein in school — i park on the street
and watch so that he knows i'm watchin
and so that he knows i know
that he knows i'm watchin

time to muscle up little crow
or be nothing but what's spent
in the makin of you

(johnny crow prays with the preacher)

minister comes to the house one day
when i am just barely asleep from the night crawlin
he says, your momma wants you to do some good
for your boy, get some kind of future,
some measure of my better nature
more than just a gesture

he says all this while i'm tryin to sleep,
layin with one eye open, thinkin he ought
to go back to baptizin babes and born agains—
i got little he may want, so i sort of shoos
him free with promises — yes lord
just as soon as i gets some sleep

he must buy it i suppose—
a promise is a man's word, and a preacher's
keen on heart-felt words — so he prays
and i listen, one hand on my head
like i too was meaning it, and intent
on the righteous
but really i keep thinkin about prayer
—like it was some great pillow,

and when he says *Amen Jesus*
i say amen jesus, just
as loud, because i'm really glad

he is done.

(johnny crow gets a girl)

she says johnny will you buy me a beer
and i say hell no buy your own damn beer
and she gets real shitty with me
like i owe some doggone thing to her

i walk over to the juke and drop
the same coins she was eyein for the beer
into the slot — i push the numbers fast,
not watchin, but smilin direct into her face

she throws a glass at me
and it splatters swill and tomato beer
all against my t-shirt
then down the length of ed's new paint

i get steamed and pick up
my own glass but ed sees it comin
and yells johnny crow get your ass
out of my bar till you sober up
and take your crazy girlfriend with you

(ain't that something)

that's the way I see the world
all in spinnin things, nothing settled
or in place permanent, all in motion,
dogs barkin drinks spillin tires squealin
knives and forks clankin against dishes
somebody else owns,
nothing quiet like snow,
nothing sleepin like tulip bulbs—
when i look out the window
i only see what is gone
beyond reach.

How Crows Find Themselves

The goldfinch bounces
lightly on the coneflower,

loops in flight
from the Rose of Sharon

to the sycamore; morning
recedes to a damp

shadow below the fence.
Doves coo—

secreted in the green.
They are conducive

to melancholia and
long thought, their sad

songs unendurable
if they weren't

forever in pairs, wings
whistling in flight.

***   ***   ***   ***

Crows on the other hand
strut the lawn

like badasses.
Even the blue jays

dance away from their
pecking. The sparrows

dart between them,
inserting into the cacophony

their hunger for
whatever seed

they can carry.
The jays rage,

demand law, curfews,
guns.

***   ***   ***   ***

By November, the wind
swings an artic fist.

There are only crows
and jays below the feeder.

The silence is rifled
with attitude.

Sparrows gather
on leafless limbs, update

Facebook posts, follow tragedy
on twitter.

How Crows Get By

So I'm out sitting by the artificial lake
just west of the city, fingering a few notes
on my Navajo courting flute, when I
hear this familiar squawking above my head.
The branches of the oaks are thick,
still full of summer leaves, but
as I crane my neck, I finally see the crow,
silhouetted on a branch.
I'm taken by his size, fat like a banker
in tails, more raven than crow.
I grin at the comedy of him,
thin legs walking a branch, head
bobbing for balance. Another crow
across the valley answers,
two squawks to his three,
gravel in a can, a Halloween rattle
spun on a black stick. I blow a bass note
from my flute. He ignores me. Answers
again the crow across the water. Heavy
acorns have been dropping all morning,
a row of geese stretch their wings
only a span above the lake. A motorcycle
guns up the park road. From beyond
the marina, children's voices cascade
the small white caps. In the nearest cove,
the water is as green as the surrounding trees,
a yellowed leaf catches air,

                              spirals to water.
I have heard that crows are thieves.
They admire sparkling necklaces,
charms, and watch fobs. They
will speak if trained, but only to mimic
our silly bird lines, a ruse for stealing
our best silver: forks, knives, spoons,
only the sterling.
Their eyes are autumn ponds,
shining like glass.

How Crows Dissolve

            The changing wind
sweeps the sky until
everything that flies has fled.

Rain finally unleashed
lashes
from the creeping gray

and only then do we run,
coats against the sky
like canvas tarps pulled
from the cinch
in our belts, we hasten

to cover the grain
of our skin,
our shoes soaked through.

In doorways
we reconnoiter, knowing
storm, the veins
of the city, traffic, gutters
swimming curb to curb
in the commerce

of crows.

We negotiate distance
to shelter, fearing that for once
we are invisible, caught
in the open, the
face we've pasted
to our forehead and cheekbones
dissolves like a cheap
mask.

Crow Remembers Cigar Bands

I wore the bastard's cigar
bands like rings. He insisted
I call him Uncle, danced us
regularly like marionettes.
Over time, my aunt
who had married in hard times,
choked in his strings, twirled
as best she could, tripped
behind his lead. His smoke
stole into every soft
cushion in the house. He kept
a small farm, sold insurance,
collected cigar boxes.

He taught captivity—
showed me how to keep
our calves from going stray
by tying a forked branch
around the leader's neck
to keep it from squeezing
between strands
of the barbed fence.

It's nearly impossible
to break a limb — green
as opposed to dead.

I could barely crease
the bark — bending,
it smoothed back
like skin, maybe
with a crease, a dent.
He twisted the branch
into a noose, jerking
his thin piston-arms
until it split
in the heart.

Fourteen Lines for Raymond Lee

Raymond Lee had a mullet until he started his lab
and then when his hair thinned he only had a photo
that ended up on the floor of his living room.
He also had a fine complexion and well-pearled teeth,
but in time his skin crawled, ragged with sores
and his teeth ended up on the floor with the picture
of his hair. But even these he couldn't keep
after the sheriff arrived one Monday night in September
and took away two women, one who claimed to be a wife
and the other who committed herself on record
as the couple's voluntary sex slave. There were no children
in the house as far as anyone could remember
just the quiet, blackened teeth that had rolled up next
to the baseboard, too far gone for rehabilitation.

A Flat Line of Crows Is Still a Murder

Uncle Raymond died when the window broke
and six crows somersaulted into the room.
Immediately, they began to strut about the recliner
on their skinny black legs, bobbing their heads
and pecking at the fragments of broken glass.
There was little rain, only a fine spray of wind
billowing the sheers and rattling the drapes.
The old Magnavox console, heavy with blue
and purple, was playing a rerun of Bonanza.
Hop Sing was in the kitchen, grappling with a large
iron skillet. Little Joe had just hung up his jacket.
Hoss was at the table, his hat still on his head.
Death came with the crash of the elm branch
and one crow stepping on the remote.

Crow's Small Wild

On the banks of the creek,
the severed wings of crows
had been fastened with baling wire
to a low limb, the small creek
trickling over the ford.
I could think of little reason
to suspend crow wings in ritual,
or as bait, or to masque man-scent.
As brittle as paper, they fluttered in
in the spring wind. We are only
a half-mile from Kansas City's
suburban sprawl, the ragged
edge where skunk and coyote
cross bean fields, scavenge
roadways and dumpsters.
Wild geese hoist their necks,
bleat at the setting sun.
A five-year-old boy digs a jawbone
from a plowed field. He swings
it like an axe
through a cloud of gnats.

Snow Dusts a Crow

If you don't notice the snow, it falls any way and it
   mounds and drifts
across the backyard. Sometimes it comes in the
   middle of the night

and you may be sleeping and not even wake until you
   hear the paperboy
swing by in his squeaking Toyota, tossing rolled
   papers over the top of the car

with a light flick of his wrist. You can have coffee in
   the morning
over a story about the day's news and drink in the
   predictions of more snow

in the afternoon. You can wade out into the gray light
and notice that along with the snow that covers the
   empty street

there's a feeling in the air
that something is expected of you.

You can sense it somewhere as part of the silence
in the cloud you breathe. It begs your attention like
   the snow

brushed from a crow's wing.

Oscar the Lab Skeleton

Old Girlfriend at Crow's Funeral

She sits on the end of the pew
and plays with the hem of her skirt.
Sorry for my loss, she says,
part of mourning, remembering

*what could have been, what
we know, who we were.*
I see our differences now, as bright
as flower arrangements, stiff

with wire, rigid with direction.
I should offer to buy her a drink
for the time lost. I'm thinking less
of the deceased, more of the woman

next to me. We are discarded
like unused Christmas wrapping,
but today she is more inviting
than the dead. I love her for that.

After Johnny's Drug Overdose Wally Keeps His Memory Alive By Begging Cookies at Truck Stops

Wally would go in
pretending to be retarded.
We'd call him Johnny,
order his food, set
his silverware, and dab
his mouth with napkins.
He'd beg like crazy
for cookies, clapping
his little seal
hands and slobbering
his Sunday special
across the table.

Begging for cookies
he'd prop
his head on the
booth cushion,
food crumbs drooling
into the lap of the
grandmother behind him.
Cookies he'd beg the
neon diner. Cookies
he'd beg the midnight
rednecks

bending coffee spoons
around middle fingers.
Cookies he'd cry
to the flabby armed
cooks and blue haired
cash register ladies.
Cookies he'd mumble
to a crooning Hank Williams
on the chrome juke.
Cookies he'd beg
for Johnny who was dead
and for the Johnnys
who lived
and for the Johnnys who were
caught
not knowing and cookieless.

And sometimes the waitresses
would feel sorry
and other times not
but when they did
they handed over cookies
like they were each
warm nippled breasts,
soft, hand-held and dipped in pink.
But we'd step in
and give them back saying

cookies ain't
good for the boy.
He's got teeth in his head
just like the rest of us.
And we'd leave him

cookieless
in the booth to pretend cry
as we walked off into the gravel parking lot
giggling at our joke.

Wally would rise
quietly like a family
man and pay the bill,
asking for his change
in just ones or fives or some odd amount,
and he might mention how
last week's rain
was just something
perfect for the milo,
and then he'd leave

everyone blank
and speechless
like a dozen open drains

and go floating off
into the night
the way Johnny did.

After Graduation Wally Rummages in the Strip Pits

He finds bonfires and bedsprings,
Windowpane and chains,
peas and carrots, cans opened, dumped
with lids awry. Rabbit fur and wind,
a cat on a trailer hitch. Lost

love, found love, love unopened. Dumped:
redemption, exemption, conscription, lawful dodging,
pectorals and biceps, anarchy and demagogues,
high spirits and rebar. Vietnam. *Crime*

and Punishment, War and Peace, Playboy, war paint,
lacquered fruit, poetry, cabinet drawers stripped
of hardware, gutted for the kitchen of dreams. Nothing
and everything sewn in a coat lining. Flying
monkeys stoned on poppies, a scarecrow, a tin man,
a lion, monopolized. Dorothy clicking her heels.

A prayer rug frayed and threadbare, legs tucked,
twisted in half lotus: sweat socks, jungle boots,
pits of alkaline, fishing line, chicken bones,
stink-bait, jail-bait and maiden-head,
draft card, milkweed and thistles. Kingfishers swinging
figure eights in an open sky. Kite string. Boots

without strings, tampons with strings, walking
on a string, promises as strings. Dragonflies
on wing. Flight. No strings attached.
The lottery: number 69.

Oily rainbows, old dogs without collars, work
without play. The beginning and the end fixed
like a fish knife, a bayonet. St. Christopher,
St. Anthony, St. Jude. (Every home
has a forwarding address.) St. Francis,
Sister Clare. A weekend with Buddhists.
Plywood, cattails, and rust,
herons and cranes and cactus spines.

A boy peering through bullet holes in a stop sign.

Wally Steals Oscar the Lab Skeleton

and props him, legs crossed,
smoking a Camel Light
in the front row
of Western Civilization 101:
6:30-7:45 MW. Night class.
He throws a scarf around
the cervical vertebrae, drapes
one end down the ribcage, the
other over the clavicle and
across the scapula, pilot like.
A note taped to the sternum
reads, *I am the 100%.*
At the window, rain lashes
from the creeping clouds;
there is lightning, thunder.
Wally makes a statement,
economics some of the issue;
he's always been broke. He
is a believer in communal
angst, ashes
to ashes, dust to dust
and all that.
Campus Security gathers
outside of Comparative
Anatomy: red lights for

the theft of bones, broken glass,
cadaver lab occupied.
Wally leans under an awning
on Cleveland Avenue, grinning
like Oscar, the joke
of a cigarette bogarted
between his teeth.

Wally Ate an Electric Hot Dog at a Rock Festival

which was laced with something
hallucinogenic. He began by shopping
for a bottle of Ripple, the line stretching
from truck to port-a-john. We found him
at dusk, flicking a cigarette lighter at the sun.
A beauty named Bambi Alvarez
danced by herself in the gloaming. A freak,
calling himself Zip, bummed all the spare change
Wally could shake out of his medicine bag
and bought himself a hot dog as well.
It was pretty much unplugged
and that saddened him. He began
to play his Bic Pen like a flute
and reciting an impromptu poem
on Jesus and Socrates and the U.S.
foreign policy. Wally rejoined us
at midnight, accompanied by a man,
with a monkey on a leash.
We weren't sure of any of this
until after the monkey escaped
and was discovered in the OD tent
making faces on some stoner's chest.
We knew this was real because the monkey
became part of a stage announcement.

Basketball Gordon poked his head
out from under a blanket he was sharing
with Bambi Alvarez, and shouted,
Free the monkey before the witch
wakes up. In the meantime, Wally
had smoked some hash he found
in the monkey's little backpack
with a cheerleader from the local high school.
She was full of bumps and giggles
and taught him to do cartwheels.

Gordon's New Age Revolution Began in a Pickup Truck

One Saturday afternoon Gordon smoked
pot in the bed of his pickup truck
with a girl from Joplin after a long
conversation about the Zodiac
and the astral plane. His mother
hasn't seen him since, but mostly
that's because of cataracts and dementia.
His father won't let him in the house
due to an outstanding debt he racked up
in the head-shop business for bongs
and hookahs and woven leather belts. So he stays
out back in a wheel-blocked Winnebago
with pole dancer Bambi Alvarez.
They have wedged cardboard
over all the windows, and grow a new
strain of Ozark Mountain Thunder Fuck
in well-lit hot water tank box,
lined with aluminum foil, anointed
with a book from Wally's library,
as plant food additive. Gordon's favorite,
an *Introduction to Zen,* adds a spiritual
osmosis to the high. Absorbing smoke
into all seven chakras
makes for better Winnebago living.

Sparrows Fly Home

Anna from Morning Glory handed out
pamphlets on birth control in her mini-skirt.
She was crowned the Anti-Queen
at Cornstalk. She turned a light on
in the art department when she tied
ribbons to sparrows, and released them
from a third story window, an act
both artistic and cruel. We climbed
a campus elm, sharing apples, nibbling
through sweetness to their arsenic seed.

I was falling in love. She was trying
not to fall from the tree. I gave her
my signed copy of *Howl.* She said, far out.
Each spring during the Military Ball,
freaks held a Peace Ball. Street people
lined the sidewalk, bumming spare change.
Anna, soaked in patchouli, gave out handfuls.
A contingent from the Cleveland Street house
smoked a box of catnip in a basement bedroom.
Anna shook her long hair over her face, meowed,
arched her back. We claimed catnip a bust,
but spent the evening playing with balls of yarn.
Anna moved back to St. Louis with a business degree.
I only saw her once after graduation. We shared
a bottle of wine the night John Lennon died.
She touched my hand, said she'd forgotten
how hard it was for birds to fly home.

Charlie Miller Burns One

Charlie drank margaritas on
the neighbor's deck and bought
his pot from a judge.
He invested in a time-share
in Colorado, but lost it
to his ex-wife, a metaphysical secretary
at Herbert & Donne. He booked
a flight to Bangladesh, and later, danced
like a Sufi at the Gurdjieff school
in Florida. He expected
some magical number seven,
some concentric circle of three
to rap out of the spiritual mall
that was 39th Street.
He met a guru with a third eye
tattooed in the center of his forehead.
He promised Charlie enlightenment
in exchange for a blowjob.
Charlie practiced vipassana in the Ozarks
with a yogi from Myanmar,
his mind settling
into soft carbon ash. He waited
for the rush to reappear
but his spirit folded, fug-bound and
blanketed in smoke. Nothing
was as simple as it used to be.

Wally Falls Asleep During Meditation Only to Be Awakened by a Home Invasion

Two large men with ski masks
forced themselves into his
little shrine room. One dropped
both knees onto his chest.
The other began duct taping
his ankles together. Blinking
rapidly and gasping for air,
Wally screwed his face into
a mask of confusion. Joke joke
he began to laugh,
what a prank, the idiocy of it,
the chaos. At some point,
as he struggled for the sake of
furthering the joke, he realized
there was a consistency to the
ski-masked faces, probably
in their dull eyes, which was
entirely devoid of humor.
In the struggle to bind his hands,
he lunged towards his altar,
burning his fingers on a stick
of sandalwood, he poked the hot end
through the knit mask, and an assailant
yelped, grabbing for his cheek
where the incense stick dangled.

His companion ripped the fake
waterfall from the Ganesh table
and smashed it into Wally's face,
river gravel flying into the corners
of the room. Wally would have
kneed him in the groin except
that his ankles were duct taped by then,
and the first guy was now
sitting on his knees, rubbing
spit from his fingers onto
his burn. That's when Wally
trepanned the second guy with the head
of his small brass Buddha. It came
to him (much as an afterthought)
that it was only thrift, a sale
in cheaply made New Age Buddhas
that saved the man's life. Silence
followed, one man rubbing his spitty,
but fragrant cheek,
the other out for the incarnation,
or so it seemed. The first leapt to his feet
and ran through the unhinged door,
the second finally moaned
and crawled on all fours after him.
Wally, although shaken, took the bus
to the local Tibetan shop
and bought a slightly taller Guan-yin.
He fashioned a Buddha holster
out of a second-hand Harley Davidson bag
and strapped it to his leg
just above his boot.

At Night, Wally Imagines the County Jail as a Monastery with Razor Wire

These walls are concrete
block, coated with Portland
cement and painted pale
green. A small stone
from the exercise yard
sits on my windowsill. I tap it
like a telegraph key, pinging
the concrete walls until
the rock vibrates

        I sit in silence and wait for an answer,

a return vibration,
        the inexplicable
                clink
        of stone against stone.

Hitching by Night across New Mexico

The river of the Milky Way flows
    above the river of the highway.
        Both stream across the desert, stretching
            from horizon to horizon.
              The hitchhiker presses

                      his thumb into a headlight's glare.
                He sucks his knuckle
            like a coyote licking a wound,
        and peers into the open window of a Buick.
The man who drives him to Amarillo
    leans into the steering wheel;

            his hands, thick with turquoise rings,
                fly like wings when he speaks,
                    the stub of his cigar
                  alive,
              silvered with spit.

Wally Reads His Second-Hand Bly at the DMV

Bly writes of a beached seal, little more
than a deflated
inner tube. All night, she drags herself

along the water's edge, the approaching tide
whispering, scraping the sand. She cannot
get close enough or far enough away

from the ocean, the inertia of her life
sweeping, sucking her back into the surf.
The opossum noses Styrofoam

at the dumpster. The closest water

a leaking garden hose, a drying culvert,
a vein of creek bed called the Turkey.
Feigning death is the 'possum's strength.

She lifts her nose above a fast food bag
like she's onto something,
stares at the grill of the passing truck.

Wally screws a new license plate
to the bumper of his Ford.

Mockingbird

One afternoon while driving home
from work, I'm almost run down
by a minivan with my hometown plates.
A friend is driving, wearing a rain hat
from our canoe trip two years ago.
He's immersed in conversation. Flies past.
My tires thump onto the shoulder.

Cleveland is losing to Kansas City
in the bottom of the sixth. My friend posts
a picture on Facebook from behind third base.
He has no clue that he almost killed me earlier.
                              Hat tipped
at a jaunty angle from the ten-dollar beers,
he appears as happy as the day
we paddled the Buffalo, summer in the water,
bird song in the air, trout shadows
on the river bottom.
Silent clouds drift above the bluff.

A fisherman on a shoal offers us a hit. He holds
a joint in his fingertips, arm outstretched.
Reefer hangs heavily in the air as our canoe
grinds ashore. The current swings the stern
until we are facing upstream. The man has a stringer
of small-mouth, glistening below the surface,
gill-strung, beating lazily into death.

Last Float Trip with Wally and the Hobbits

Rain and sleet pelted
the crocus, popped
off the flotsam of spring.
Our john boat
slugged through the waves,
took on water,
and foundered. We bailed
with a plastic Clorox jug
until it, too, escaped beyond
reach. The boat swamped
before it capsized,
spilling us in a willow jungle,
the flat bottom
inverted, disappearing
behind a snag of limb fall,
bobbers, and fishing line.
No one could say
we hadn't seen it coming,
the water and the boat
drawing heavily, becoming one.
We paddled in small circles,
gripping our warden pipes,
hollering across the icy water,
the flood spinning us away
from each other like leaves.

Highway Signs Are Painted Green

On Saturday, Anna left her husband and her
    boyfriend with a symbolic flourish.
She had tossed her belongings in a box
and covered them with a tarp.
Not owning much kept it simple. It was no trouble
to slide the box in the trunk of her boyfriend's car and
    let him drive her
to their usual motel. Neither the boyfriend nor her
    husband Phil suspected much,

but by midnight after she crushed a Xanax in her
    boyfriend's beer,
she was thirty miles south on the interstate to Tulsa.
    A note
on the night stand consisted of a simple grocery list
in green ink on a motel notepad.

Would you pick these items up at the IGA
and take them to Phil? Tell him
all that you wished I'd said to you. Thank you
for the green blouse you bought from Target.
It matched the color of the eyes I always wished I had.

The Day Wally Was Murdered Love Poem

She came at him
with a knife
and drove it
into his upper
left pectoral
muscle. It was
only a rubber knife
with a painted
silver blade. But
she put some
umpff into it.
He knew the knife
a fake before
she lunged, so he
wasn't scared,
really, more startled
by the blaze
in her eyes.
She was crazy
with her desire
to stab him
with something,

even rubber,
folding what

the fuck
up to the hilt,
up to her fist,
through his upper
ribcage, nearly
missing the
spot, where
she insisted,
he had
no heart.

Wally Dismisses Crises by Shooting an Inanimate Object

For two months I lived in a broken-down bus
behind a friend's house. I went out a lot, especially
when daylight savings time ended and the weather
turned. Mostly, I was miserable. Confident
in little. I kept two lawn chairs outside
the door of the bus. On warm afternoons I entertained
the thought of guests. Like in an intermission,
we'd watch the crows along the creek bed.
A cemetery bordered the backyard, and as the trees
lost their leaves throughout November,
the marbles became more visible. Often, their slant
would be the last light I saw before sliding the door shut,
igniting the Coleman catalytic, and crawling
into my sleeping bag to read Hemingway by flashlight.

One Saturday night after doling bourbon
into a coffee mug, I decided that I'd shivered enough
from dusk to dawn. I borrowed a friend's pistol (an antique
he insisted), and I aimed directly between the headlights.
The wound was anti-climactic, a small dent
next to the VW emblem, no sparks, no gaping hole—
just a small crease in the silence.

After the Book Release Party, Wally Walks Down 39th Street with a Box on His Head

For a moment, he is the only
one on the street, then a waitress
steps out of Jazz
and lights a cigarette. Her smoke
jets skyward into the falling snow.
He tells her there is a poem in this
and he waves his free arm
into the silence of snow.
She lifts her chin in recognition;
the smoke curls from her
lips into her nose. To his myopic eyes
snowflakes streak the sky
like an impressionist's brush strokes—
shops closed, neon smudged like
daubs on a pallet. The gray slush
is slick underfoot. If he falls,
volumes of unsold poems
will spill to his feet.
One of them is a sonnet
about his mother at the nursing home.
In fourteen lines he tells
how she remembers him, or at least,
someone similar to him,
who grew old and blank
and one winter night walked
off behind the 7-11
and forgot to return.

Old Boy

Wally didn't own a shotgun, but he'd
recently found three tennis rackets
in a dumpster behind the sport's club.

They were wooden, still strung with catgut,
one had a sweat stained leather grip.
All three were perfect for hunting ducks.

When Wally applied for his duck stamp,
the state said, what the hell do you mean
you're going to hunt ducks with a racket?

What kind of ducks, pintails, canvasbacks?
Wally replied that one duck was
as good as the next, but he preferred fowl

that flew within three feet of his blind, those
slower than the rest who had
grown apathetic to migration, and were

content to laze around the refuge, semi-
retired and prone to windy monologues
on the plump hens they'd known.

Wally's Professor Busts a Local Meth Lab

The professor was known to lose track of himself for
hours on end. New Year's Eve was no exception.
He had merely driven one block too far to a departmental
cocktail and had consequently knocked on the door
of a meth lab. The junkie with the forty-five
told police in his subsequent six-hour stand-off that
he had no intention of shooting a professor that night;
it was an accident forced by improper residential
zoning. Professors he insisted shouldn't be barging in
on the privacy of a lab; recipes are arguably intellectual
property. The girlfriend, still doe-eyed, but lined
and creased with hard riding peeked from behind the
gun. Doyle, she said, nudging her boyfriend with her
forehead. That's the professor who flunked me out of
English 101. We got nowhere to run.

The After Midnight Super Market

A man studies the potato chip rack
for several minutes before selecting
the right bag of corn chips. He's
bent in the lower back and walks
with a tilt to his right side. Probably,
he has not spoken to anyone
at the super market for years.
When I step between him and the
puffed Cheetos, he limps hurriedly
toward Soup/Canned Meat. I'm left
holding a container of artichoke dip.

Cucumbers are mixed in the zucchini bin
and I need some help telling one
from the other. A dark haired woman
shucks an ear of sweet corn with quick
deft hands. I come up behind her
with my cucumber/zucchini. I think
how awkward this could be for her.
I say nothing, back away into the
yellow onions. On my cell phone
I google cucumber/zucchini.
The website asks if I'm 21 years old.

The butcher and I talk tabloids
while he mashes ground beef
into a one-pound loaf with his fist.
This is where it all goes down:
knives, cleavers, bone saws, dark
hooks from the ceiling.
He wears plastic gloves, a ball cap,
a blood splattered white jacket.
Before long I'm telling him
everything I know, spilling my guts
about Big Foot, Bat Boy and UFOs.

Dancing at the American Legion

Vietnam Was Once

A previously unpublished 20-minute
impromptu poem by a famous poet
is lost somewhere between Pittsburg, Kansas,
and Los Angeles, California.
A cassette tape recorded live
an hour before the cocktails,
the smart talk, the back-porch reefer.
If you should stumble upon it in a box
at a Salvation Army or in a flea market stall,
don't erase, there is no other
like it on the planet.

You see, there was Vietnam and Agent Orange
and who could have guessed cancer and recovery
and alcohol and pot and lovely hippie girls
and children and marriage
and divorce and a loss of possessions
(of which there were few),
a mudslide that began on the summer of Tet
and ended one Halloween
in Kansas. There was

homelessness: poems, pants, shirts,
underwear in a brown bag,
then more alcohol and the loss of the few

remaining loyal friends
and estrangement
from children and grandchildren
and the terrible loneliness of dreams
tossed like a pink slip from a speeding GTO,
and somewhere in the middle of this love-hate
inverted pyramid balancing act of it all,
there was a moment in the back of mother's garage
when the thought of the cassette tape
rewound itself, played for just a moment
in the blue alcohol misery haze.
This was once.

And it was impossible to imagine
retracing the steps that led to this cardboard box
that you had packed and unpacked and repacked
through the moves from house to apartment
to car to shelter to Kansas again, more times
than you can count in the this-is-once juggling act,
even if you wanted to, even if you wanted to know
the numbers of your loss, even if you knew
that being here in Kansas now

was no way near the here you sought then,
when once you set the recorder between your feet,
the microphone pressed between your knees,
the poem dancing electric between your ears,
and all this, knowing in the beginning,

when you were sure, cocksure,
that the journey to paradise
wouldn't lead to just another fucked-up bus stop dream.
The famous poet asked over coffee,
did you get the poem recorded,
and you said you did, grainy and dim,
blanketed by coughs and scraping feet,
but recorded, yes, you did.
He asked for a copy and took out a buck.
You said you'd mail it to him
and took his secret address.
This was once.

Screwing the Pooch

Last night I dreamed
that in a moment of hubris
I punched my boss in the face.
Of course, that was the end
of my career. Well-connected,
he made sure I never found
employment in women's
under garments again,
which I thought didn't matter
since I was old and near
retirement. But then my blue
truck got stolen, and I spent
much of the night searching
parking lots and garages.
Witnesses weren't talking. They
kept the whereabouts of
my ride close to their vests.
I was late for the new job
at the Bingo Hall. I phoned
to explain myself. My boss
wouldn't take my call.
I'd screwed the pooch. At home,
back in my parent's house,
my father gave me that look
I'd feared as a kid. My mother

set a platter of pancakes
on the table before closing
the door in my face.
My lovely girlfriend wept
as she rode away on the back
of Gordon's banana seat.

The Hat Trick

I woke in the early morning
before the sun had risen
feeling stupid. Stupid for not

accepting earlier, when
I turned out the light from
the blank page, that I was

little more than a cafe
magician working tables,
groveling through an old hat

for a fucking rabbit,
the same rabbit every time,
hidden well behind

the sweat band, a size 7
&3/8 parlor trick. Last week
I lay my hat down

on a box of poetry journals
at my garage sale, and some
early riser with 5 dollars

tried to buy the hat.
The 10-dollar price tag,
obviously faded,

was still in place, and although
this was half-off day,
my fondness for rabbits

would not let it go. Maybe,
a rule of business, a sense
that even a rabbit in a hat

deserves two weeks' notice,
thirty days at the most,
for cash in hand.

Wally Recalls Maslow's Hierarchy

Last night Wally ate four hamburger sliders.
They were smeared in ketchup, mustard
and grilled onions. He cut the grease
with a swallow of light beer
and wiped his hands on his Levi's.

In the back of the bar was this rode-hard woman
shooting pool. He'd seen her before at the Walmart.
She aimed her finger at him like it was a pistol
and then blew the smoke away. Wally
couldn't tell if that was a good sign or not,
so he did the same. She feigned impact,
the finger bullet striking her in the shoulder.
She flipped backwards onto the pool table,
Scattering balls in a solid break.
Her partner helped her up and glared at Wally
for using a loaded finger in a public place.
This is a family establishment he bellowed.
Wally shot again.

The imaginary bullet went wide and struck
a *Miller Lite* sign. If the bullet hadn't been a figment,
the sign would have shattered, sending little shards
of plastic and electricity into the far corners
of the bar. People cleared a path,
barstools clattering to the floor.

The older beauty chalked her pool cue
and stepped between them. Secretly, she loved
having men fight over her. It hadn't happened
for years, and for a time, she felt sexy
like the deep blue lights
inside of the jukebox. Wally figured *no blood
no foul,* so he sent the two an order
of hamburger sliders. The man gave
the woman a knuckle punch
and they racked up the balls like nothing had happened.
Wally abhorred violence, so he stacked his
empty plate with other empty plates
and holstered his finger, promising
never to wield it again, unless he was called out.
Then, by God, enough was enough.

Prayer Feet

We are all dying — the mud of our bodies,
cracking, falling as dust off our shoes.
We wear the Birkenstocks of saints
and bodhisattvas — leather, canvas, hemp,
tire-treaded soles. We are mud. We are dust.
We are Shiva the Destroyer, Vishnu the Preserver.
Barefoot Buddha. Foot washing Jesus.
We choose the shoes we wear, mud-caked
and dying like Moses when he walked
out on Pharaoh, climbed Mt. Sinai.
(Gettysburg began as a raid on a shoe factory.)
The Kabbalist in black wingtips claims
to see in part, only in part — the strings, the toe,
the heel, the sole. St. Francis barefoot
gives away his sandals like alms, coins to lepers.
We wear slip-on Toms, mountain Vasques,
steel-toed Redwings, rubber Crocs. We are
the mud dried on evangelist's tongues, flaked
into dust, walked on by those still coming
and those still coming after them. We are
footprints to the future for those who come up
from behind and from further behind still come,
looking or not looking, they find us the same.
Cool river, we squeeze our toes into the sandy bottom,
slop in the ooze that dries on the bank.

O First face. Zen face. Today I don't feel well.
Probably I am dying. I've seen Nikes in the city,
Doc Martins on the hip, engraved silver on Tony Lama's,
discarded sneakers flung faithfully
over telephone wires. Just as me, just as you
wear shoes to prevent falling, bruises, lacerations—
O pain. O gout. O corns. O plantar fasciitis.
Sisyphus stubs his toe on the mountain. Gandhi
climbs ice in spiritual crampons. Kierkegaard
pinched by too tight brogans
sings melancholy love songs, hunchbacked,
down in the heel. Michelangelo
springs up ladders in winged sandals. Dali
preens in toe shoes. Combat boots
for miniskirts. Jungle boots
for hobnail souls. Looking first behind,
then ahead. We step out in prayer feet
—like a parade of mornings
stepping out and stepping out again.

Dancing at the American Legion

A one-armed man
dances to 60s music
at a local bar. He moves
completely in time
with the beat of the song.
When he turns in the beer light,
his partner twirls easily through the neon.
She knows where his hand should be
if he had a hand at the end
of where his arm once was.
For a while tonight, nothing has changed.
She swings her hips with his,
spins out across the dance floor,
rolls back in towards him,
turns once into the crook of his shoulder.
They are both smiling, sweating
in fluid happiness. Tonight,
there is no phantom pain, no itch
in the invisible palm. No
absence of a lifeline.

Wally Practices Pranayama at the Self-Serve

I stop at the local self-serve
to pump a tank of gas
and visit with my friend
from the Punjab. He stands
behind the glass window
and after doling out change
explains pranayama,
the shelves thick with incense,
bath salts, cigarette papers,
disposable lighters. He presses
his thumb over one nostril
and breathes. He switches
thumb and nostril. *Only
minutes a day,* he insists,
*and in forty days even your
glaucoma will improve.*

In fact, just across
the parking lot, there is an
acupuncturist. Very famous
for her work. *Asian?* I ask.
He nods, *yes, the Chinese
know it best. A thousand,
two thousand years. Longer.*
Behind the pork rinds, the
Jack Links, the sunflower
seeds are lined jugs
of windshield cleaner
as blue as the bluest sky.

Wally Sings Amazing Grace in an Arkansas Cave

The old timers drew
arrows with carbide smoke
to mark their return.
Two caves, they used
to say, one going in,
one going out.

You stop for granola,
raisins, apple slices.
You wander the deep transept,
searching the source
of breeze on your cheek,
hunting new cave, tight
spots, wiggle room.
The darkness becomes
more personal, pressing—
brown bat, albino fish,
blind to sun.
Wally begins *Amazing Grace*.
The rope of his voice
belayed through the darkness
like a bowline at your waist—
the mist in your lamp,
the scalloped walls
curving on.

When you leave work today,
you walk through snow melt,
your truck parked at the bottom

of the corporate lot. Gray drifts
run in small creeks to the
gutter. At the storm drain,
the water sluices through
concrete to a distant spillway.
This too is cave, piped below
the streets, subterranean,
serene, even rat trod,
it's a river to the sea.

The Starving Mule

It was a night so cold
that the stars shivered
high up in their black hole
orbits. They shimmered
like shards of ice, and we felt
all the sadder for them.
The mule wasn't starving
for oats or carrots
or some feedbag recipe,
but for other-mule attention.
At least, that's what
the cowboy said, as he
circled in next to the fire,
still shaking from the
startle he'd taken, the mule
leaping up out of the hay pile
just as the cowboy was leaning in
to grab an armful of bedding.
The night was due to drop
even colder before dawn,
and whatever it took, stuffed
below the sleeping bag,
slowed the chill that seeped
up through the caprock.
The mule had known as much,

but not much more. He could
have joined the cowboy
in our circle around the fire,
had a pull of Jack Black,
told a mule story, cracked an ass joke.
We might have stared at him curiously,
at first, but only till we got acquainted.
Possibly, his shy nature was simply
too abject, and that forced him
to flee among the scrub oaks
on an unfriendly night. The cowboy
said this after a bit, the mule
looming like an archetype
in his mind. He went on,
speaking mostly to himself,
that the mule, any equine
for that matter, in choosing
the devil that he knew, starved
for better information.

Wally Smokes a Cigar with Sam Clemens

Wally disappeared shortly after buying his first smart phone. I guess he felt there was little else he could contribute to a world with such quick reflexes. When his aunt called me to sort through the trailer where Wally kept his things, I came upon this manuscript of old poems. Some were completed, others were in the shape of cats, skirting through night shadows. I liberated as many as I could from years of mildew and set them up in a Word file.

The last any of us heard, Wally had traveled to northern Minnesota, sold his Ford, and purchased a rundown house boat. His purported goal, according to the used boat salesman at Mike's Marina, was to float the Mississippi from its headwaters near Bemidji to its mouth in New Orleans. He carried with him an old Royal typewriter and an array of musical instruments. His only book was a well-thumbed copy of *Huckleberry Finn*.

Al Ortolani's poetry has appeared in journals such as *Rattle, Prairie Schooner*, and *Tar River Poetry*. His newest collection, *On the Chicopee Spur,* has just been released from New York Quarterly Books. A previous collection, *Ghost Sign,* Spartan Press/39 West, co-authored with J.T. Knoll, Adam Jameson, and Melissa Fite Johnson was selected as a Kansas Notable Book for 2017. Ortolani is the Manuscript Editor for Woodley Press in Topeka, Kansas, and directs a memoir writing project for Vietnam veterans across Kansas in association with the Library of Congress and Humanities Kansas. He currently lives in the Kansas City area.

This project was made possible, in part, by generous support from the Osage Arts Community.

Osage Arts Community provides temporary time, space and support for the creation of new artistic works in a retreat format, serving creative people of all kinds — visual artists, composers, poets, fiction and nonfiction writers. Located on a 152-acre farm in an isolated rural mountainside setting in Central Missouri and bordered by ¾ of a mile of the Gasconade River, OAC provides residencies to those working alone, as well as welcoming collaborative teams, offering living space and workspace in a country environment to emerging and mid-career artists. For more information, visit us at www.osageac.org

www.ingramcontent.com/pod-product-compliance
Lightning Source LLC
Chambersburg PA
CBHW030119100526
44591CB00009B/460